RACE TO THE MOON

EXPEDITION

THE STORY OF APOLLO 11

EXPEDITION

EDITOR APRIL McCROSKIE
Technical Advisor Mark Whitchurch

An SBC Book, created, designed, and produced by
The Salariya Book Company
25 Marlborough Place
Brighton
East Sussex
BN1 1UB

Franklin Watts 1998
First American Edition by
Franklin Watts
A Division of Grolier Publishing
90 Sherman Turnpike
Danbury, CT 06816

ISBN 0-531-14456-9

A copy of the Cataloging-in-Publication data is
available from the Library of Congress

Visit Franklin Watts on the Internet at:
http://publishing. grolier.com

JEN GREEN
graduated from the University of Sussex with a PhD in
English Literature in 1982. She has worked as an editor
and manager in children's publishing for 15 years and
is now a full-time writer. She has written many books
for children.
For Hannah and Edward, JG.

MARK BERGIN
was born in Hastings in 1961. He studied at
Eastbourne College of Art and has specialized in
historical reconstruction since leaving art school in
1983. He lives in Sussex with his wife and children.
For Hannah, Isabelle and Edward, MB.

DAVID SALARIYA
was born in Dundee, Scotland. He has designed and
created many new series of children's books. In 1989,
he established The Salariya Book Company Ltd.
He lives in Brighton with his wife, the illustrator
Shirley Willis, and their son Jonathan.

RACE TO THE MOON

The Story of Apollo 11

Written by JEN GREEN

Illustrated by MARK BERGIN

Created and designed by
DAVID SALARIYA

W
FRANKLIN WATTS
A Division of Grolier Publishing
NEW YORK • LONDON • HONG KONG • SYDNEY
DANBURY, CONNECTICUT

CONTENTS

EXPEDITION

INTRODUCTION

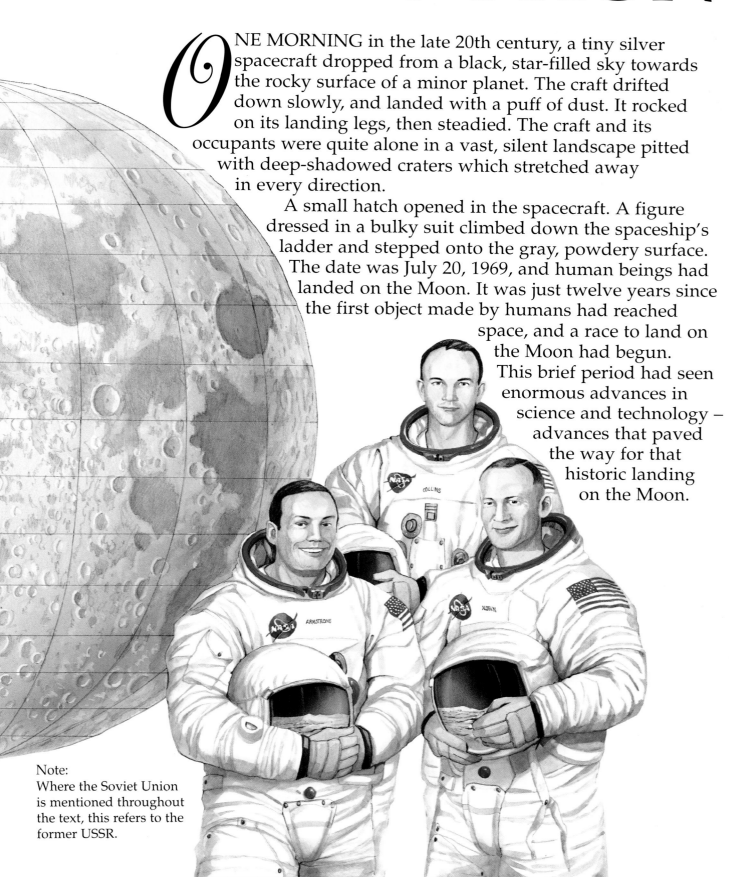

ONE MORNING in the late 20th century, a tiny silver spacecraft dropped from a black, star-filled sky towards the rocky surface of a minor planet. The craft drifted down slowly, and landed with a puff of dust. It rocked on its landing legs, then steadied. The craft and its occupants were quite alone in a vast, silent landscape pitted with deep-shadowed craters which stretched away in every direction.

A small hatch opened in the spacecraft. A figure dressed in a bulky suit climbed down the spaceship's ladder and stepped onto the gray, powdery surface. The date was July 20, 1969, and human beings had landed on the Moon. It was just twelve years since the first object made by humans had reached space, and a race to land on the Moon had begun. This brief period had seen enormous advances in science and technology – advances that paved the way for that historic landing on the Moon.

Note:
Where the Soviet Union is mentioned throughout the text, this refers to the former USSR.

The First Rockets
Rockets were invented in China about 2,000 years ago. They were used as weapons against the Mongol army that invaded China in AD 1232. For the next 500 years rockets were used as fireworks and as weapons.

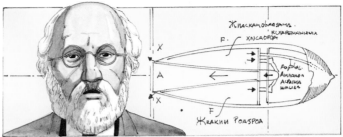

Tsiolkovsky's Idea
The father of modern space travel was Konstantin Tsiolkovsky, a Russian inventor. In 1903 he suggested that liquid fuel should be used to power rockets, since it could be controlled more easily than solid fuel.

HUNDREDS OF YEARS before astronauts set foot on the Moon, a few people dreamed of traveling through space. But it was not until the early 20th century that a Russian inventor, Konstantin Tsiolkovsky, thought of using rockets to reach space. An American scientist, Robert Goddard, was the first to build and launch a successful rocket, in 1926.

During World War II, the German army used rockets to launch bombs under the supervision of a scientist named Wernher von Braun. After the war, von Braun went to live in America. He was to mastermind the American space program, including the Apollo launches.

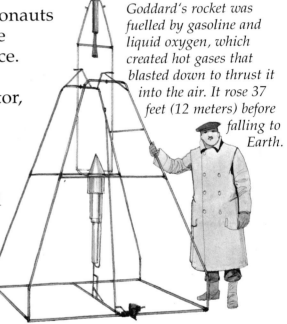

Goddard's rocket was fuelled by gasoline and liquid oxygen, which created hot gases that blasted down to thrust it into the air. It rose 37 feet (12 meters) before falling to Earth.

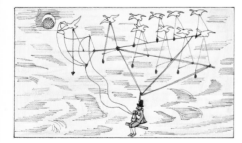

Space Dreams
In the 16th century, an author named Francis Godwin wrote a story about a trip to the Moon. The hero was towed there by a team of wild swans.

Science Fiction
In 1865 French author, Jules Verne, wrote a science fiction book about a journey to the Moon. His book inspired scientists such as von Braun.

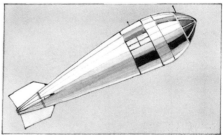

Rocket Stages
Tsiolkovsky thought Earth's gravity could be overcome by using rockets, arranged in stages so they could take over from each other.

•DREAMS OF SPACE TRAVEL•

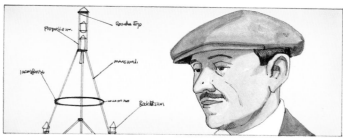

Goddard's Rocket

An American scientist, Robert Goddard, built the first high-altitude rocket in 1926. Like Tsiolkovsky, Goddard realized that only a rocket that could carry all its own fuel could escape Earth's gravity to reach space.

Vengeance Weapon

During World War II a scientist named Wernher von Braun developed a rocket-powered missile in Germany. It was called the V-2, or vengeance weapon.

During World War II Germany launched V-2 rockets carrying explosives. Over 1,400 rockets were fired at London. Following Tsiolkovsky's theory, they burned liquid fuel. When Germany was defeated in 1945, von Braun surrendered to the United States army and became an American citizen.

Moon Myths

For centuries stargazers have marveled at the Moon in the sky. To the ancient Egyptians, the Moon was the symbol of Thoth, god of wisdom.

Man in the Moon

Throughout history the craters on the Moon's surface suggested to people the shapes of animals such as a hare, or a giant human face.

Little Green Men

The idea that the Moon might be inhabited by aliens has persisted into the 20th century, and inspired many science fiction films.

•FIRST IN SPACE•

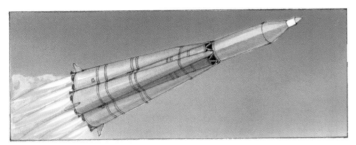

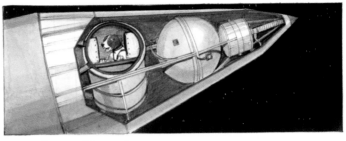

The Space Age Begins
The Soviet space program was led by a brilliant scientist, Sergei Korolyev. By 1957 the Soviets had built a powerful rocket, the SS-6. On October 4, the rocket was used to place a satellite, *Sputnik 1*, in orbit round the Earth.

First Space Traveler
In November 1957 the Soviets followed this success with another impressive first. A second, larger satellite, *Sputnik 2*, carried a dog called Laika into space. Unfortunately Laika did not survive her trip.

A PERIOD OF HOSTILITY between the Soviet Union and the United States began after World War II. This was known as the Cold War. The two countries wanted to show that their scientists were making great advances (and so would be capable of making new and terrible weapons). Americans believed their technology was superior, and so were shocked when, in 1957, the Soviets shot a satellite, *Sputnik 1*, into space. Soon a second triumph was announced: the Soviets had put a man, Yuri Gagarin, in space.

A new powerful Soviet rocket was used to launch Gagarin into space. His spacecraft Vostok ("East") 1, was a round capsule on top of an instrument section with rockets which fired to control the craft's position.

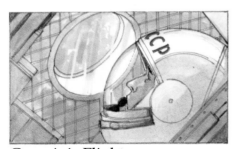

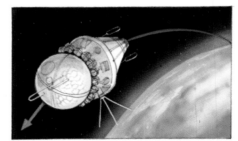

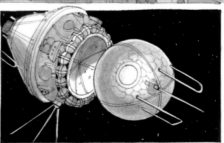

Gagarin's Flight
As he was blasted into the atmosphere in *Vostok 1*, Gagarin had a unique view of the Earth as it fell away beneath him.

In Orbit
Vostok 1 orbited the Earth at over 16, 200 miles (27,000 kilometers) an hour, flying over India, Australia, and Africa.

Re-Entry
As the re-entry sequence began, Gagarin's craft had to enter Earth's atmosphere at exactly the right speed and angle, to avoid burning up.

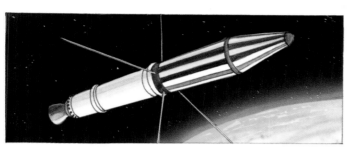

American Launch
American attempts to match the Soviets failed. After a navy rocket exploded on the launch pad, von Braun was called in to design America's rockets. In 1958 he launched the first American satellite, *Explorer 1*.

Man in Space
On April 12, 1961, after more test flights with dogs, the Soviets put the first man in space. Major Yuri Gagarin was the first "cosmonaut" – the Russian word for astronaut. He made a single orbit of the Earth.

A satellite is an object, natural or manufactured, orbiting (circling) another in space. The Moon is a satellite of the Earth. The first manufactured satellite, Sputnik 1, was a small metal sphere containing a radio transmitter. Long aerials were attached to the sphere, which weighed 185 pounds (84 kilograms), as much as a heavy person. Sputnik ("Traveler") orbited the Earth for 92 days before burning up.

Fireball
The capsule glowed with heat as it entered the atmosphere. Gagarin experienced powerful forces called G forces as his craft slowed down.

Ejection
Gagarin ejected at 23,100 feet (7,000 meters). At the time the Soviets claimed he had not ejected, to make the flight sound even more impressive.

Safe Landing
Gagarin's parachute brought him down to Earth near the River Volga in Russia. His craft also landed safely using parachutes.

Americans in Space

In 1961 the first American astronaut, Alan Shepard, entered space. The following year John Glenn became the first American to orbit the Earth. He completed three circuits before splashing down in the Atlantic Ocean.

First Woman Cosmonaut

In 1963 the Soviets pressed forward again; Valentina Tereshkova became the first woman in space. She spent almost three days in space, completing 48 orbits. Her spacecraft liaised with another Soviet craft.

Following President Kennedy's speech in 1961, the Moon landing project, code-named Apollo, *was given massive funding.*

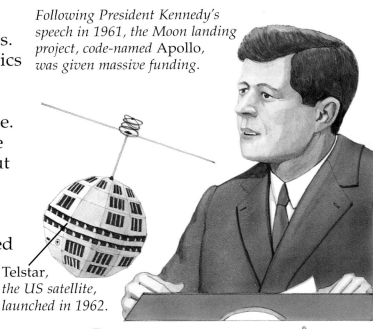

Telstar, *the US satellite, launched in 1962.*

GAGARIN'S SUCCESS embarrassed the United States. America's National Aeronautics and Space Administration (NASA) had been formed in 1958: its aim was to put a man in space. By 1961 NASA had sent a chimpanzee named Ham on a brief space flight, but while von Braun was perfecting the American rocket, news came of Gagarin's success. In May 1961 the new president, John F. Kennedy, vowed that America would place a man on the Moon and return him safely to Earth before 1970. The race was on.

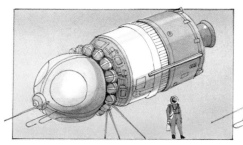

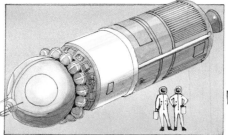

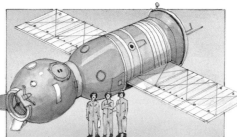

Soviet Spacecraft
1. Vostok
During the 1960s the Soviets developed three craft for use in space. *Vostok* was the first Soviet spacecraft.

2. Voskhod
By 1964 the Soviets had altered the design of *Vostok* to produce *Voskhod*, which could carry three cosmonauts in very cramped conditions.

3. Soyuz
The Soviets launched a new craft, *Soyuz* ("Union") in 1967. The first mission ended in disaster when the craft crashed after 18 orbits.

•SOVIETS LEAD IN SPACE EXPLORATION•

Cosmonauts in "Shirt-Sleeves"
In 1964 the Soviets launched *Voskhod 1* (*"Sunrise"*) which carried three cosmonauts in a cabin filled with air, so there was no need for spacesuits.

First Walk in Space
In 1965 Russian cosmonaut Alexei Leonov took the first "walk" in space. On re-entry his craft landed 1,920 miles (3,200 kilometers) off course and the crew had to spend a night surrounded by wolves before rescue came!

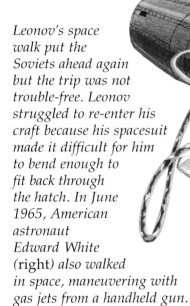

Leonov's space walk put the Soviets ahead again but the trip was not trouble-free. Leonov struggled to re-enter his craft because his spacesuit made it difficult for him to bend enough to fit back through the hatch. In June 1965, American astronaut Edward White (right) also walked in space, maneuvering with gas jets from a handheld gun.

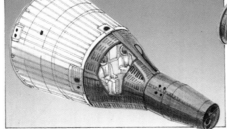

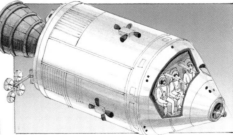

American Spacecraft
1. Mercury
The first American spaceships were *Mercury* capsules. They were used for space missions from 1961-1963.

2. Gemini
Two-person *Geminis* replaced *Mercury* craft in 1965. Astronauts controlled the craft themselves and practiced maneuvering in space.

3. Apollo
Although the *Apollo* space program began in 1963, the first *Apollo* craft did not get off the ground until 1968.

• AMERICA CATCHES UP •

Docking Practice
During 1965-69 American astronauts practiced for the Moon mission in *Gemini* craft. Two *Apollo* craft would need to meet and dock (join) in space. In 1965 *Geminis 5* and *6* flew within yards of each other.

Launch Pad Disaster
In 1967 the *Apollo* project was struck by disaster. Three astronauts died when fire broke out in their capsule on the launch pad. The materials used in the craft were quickly changed to make it less likely to catch fire.

SO, by the early 1960s, America and the Soviet Union were racing one another to the Moon. The *Apollo* spaceship designed by the Americans consisted of two craft which could fly together but also operate separately: a command ship and a Moon lander. The Moon lander would visit the Moon and then rejoin the main ship for the trip back to Earth. A new rocket would be needed to carry the craft into space. But there were questions about the Moon itself. Was the surface suitable for landing, or was it covered with a layer of dust which a spacecraft would sink into? Both countries sent unmanned craft, called probes, to investigate.

American probe, Surveyor 3.

"Phases" of the Moon
As the Moon orbits the Earth, we can see more or less of the side that is lit by the Sun. This makes the Moon appear to change shape.

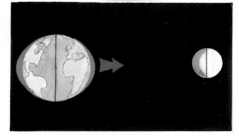

Force of Gravity
The pull of Earth's gravity on the Moon keeps it in orbit around us. The Moon's gravity pulls the oceans on our planet, causing tides.

Distant World
The Moon is 230,640 miles (384,400 kilometers) from Earth. It took *Apollo 8* three days to reach it.

•THE EARLY YEARS OF APOLLO•

Apollo 8

In December 1968 *Apollo 8* lifted off on a mission vital to the program. On board Frank Borman, Jim Lovell, and Bill Anders were the first men to leave Earth's orbit and start traveling to the Moon.

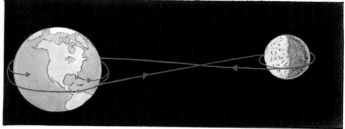

Far Side of the Moon

The *Apollo 8* astronauts were the first to see the far side of the Moon, on Christmas Eve, 1968. The crew spent 20 hours orbiting the Moon before returning safely to Earth and splashing down in the Pacific Ocean.

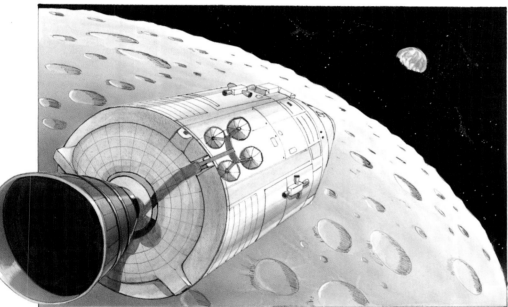

On the Moon's far side, the crew of Apollo 8 lost contact with NASA when the bulk of the Moon blocked out radio signals. Everyone at Mission Control center in Houston, Texas, waited anxiously for the ship to clear the far side and re-establish contact. The mission went without a hitch and returned safely.

"Seas" on the Moon

Dark areas on the Moon are known as "seas." In fact they are waterless plains, formed by lava from volcanoes, now extinct (no longer active).

Struck by Meteors

The great craters which can be seen on the Moon were caused by meteors (giant rocks) crashing into the Moon's surface.

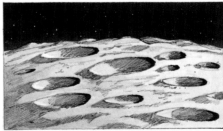

No Atmosphere

The gases of Earth's atmosphere protect us from the Sun. Without atmosphere the Moon is scorching hot by day, and freezing at night.

•DESTINATION: MOON•

The Early Apollos

The first six *Apollo* missions were designed to test von Braun's new Saturn rocket and were unmanned. In March 1969 *Apollo 9* astronauts practiced docking the command ship with the lunar module in Earth's orbit.

Apollo 10

The *Apollo 10* mission was planned to test the lunar module in orbit round the Moon. Only if it was completely successful would the Moon landing go ahead. In May 1969 *Apollo 10* lifted off and headed for the Moon.

I

N 1969 *Apollo 11* was named as the craft scheduled to make the Moon landing. It consisted of three parts, or modules. The command module was nicknamed *Columbia* and would carry the astronauts for most of the journey and return with them to Earth.

Mission badge

The three stages of the Saturn 5 rocket (right).

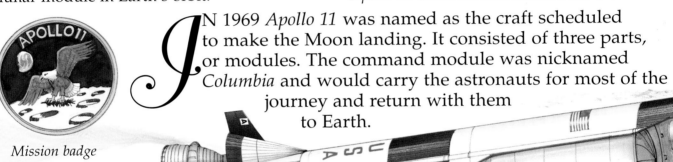

Five engines

First stage

Engines

The Astronauts
Neil Armstrong
Neil Armstrong had been a pilot in the Korean War. He commanded the *Gemini 8* mission in 1966.

Buzz Aldrin
Edwin ("Buzz") Aldrin had also been a pilot in Korea. In 1966 he had piloted *Gemini 12* and walked in space for over two hours, a record time.

Michael Collins
Michael Collins had flown in *Gemini 10* in 1966. The men picked for the *Apollo 11* flight were all experienced pilots. All three were born in 1930.

Landing Practice
As part of the test-flight two astronauts in *Apollo 10*'s lunar module descended to within 47,718 feet (14,460 meters) of the Moon's surface, but did not land. Instead they rejoined the main ship and returned to Earth.

Soviet Moon Mission
Three days before the launch of *Apollo 11*, the Soviet Union sent a spacecraft, *Luna 15*, on a mysterious Moon mission. It may have been designed to collect rock samples, but in fact it crashed on the Moon and broke up.

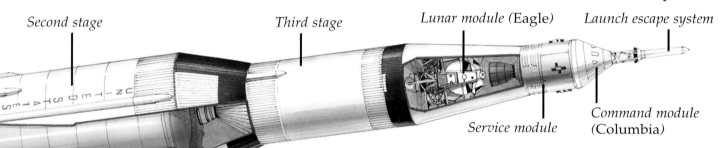

Second stage   *Third stage*   *Lunar module* (Eagle)   *Launch escape system*

Service module   *Command module* (Columbia)

Attached to *Columbia* was the service module which housed the rockets and fuel that would be needed for the round trip to the Moon. The lunar module (*Eagle*) would take two of the astronauts down to the Moon. After they had explored the surface, the *Eagle*'s rockets would fire to carry them back to *Columbia*, orbiting above.

The Apollo craft was so heavy von Braun had to design the largest rocket ever built, Saturn 5, to blast it into space. It stood 366 feet (111 meters) tall and was assembled at Cape Canaveral, Florida, in a building so tall that clouds sometimes gathered at the top at night. The rocket burned a mixture of kerosene and liquid oxygen.

In Training
Before the mission the three astronauts practiced every move in machines called simulators which worked just like the *Apollo* craft.

Weightlessness
Once clear of Earth's gravity, all astronauts experience weightless conditions. Aldrin, Armstrong, and Collins trained underwater for this.

Like Outer Space
Weightless conditions can also be experienced inside aircraft flying special curved paths. On these flights the astronauts practiced moving around.

•WE HAVE LIFT-OFF! •

Early Call
The morning of July 16, dawned clear and bright. The astronauts ate a large breakfast of steak, eggs, toast, orange juice, and coffee at Cape Canaveral. Then they were driven across the base to the launch pad.

On the Launch Pad
The *Saturn 5* rocket towered high above the launch pad. The astronauts were taken to the top in the launch tower lift. From the top they could see the Atlantic Ocean glinting beyond the marshland of the cape.

L AUNCH DAY for *Apollo 11*'s mission was July 16, 1969. Two hours before take-off the three astronauts took their seats in the command module. Buzz Aldrin, who would help fly the lunar module, sat in the center. On Aldrin's left was Neil Armstrong, the flight commander. He would be the first to step on the Moon. On his right sat Michael Collins, the command module pilot, who would stay on board. The countdown went smoothly, and soon after 9:30AM, amid a cloud of flaming gas and steam, *Apollo 11* roared into the air.

Mission Control in Houston, Texas (above).

Ready for Launch
At 9:32AM *Apollo 11* was cleared for take-off. It had taken over five hours to fill the rocket's tanks with 2,000 tons of explosive fuel.

Ignition
As the engines ignited, a huge ball of orange flame appeared around the rocket's base. The ground shook as the rocket cleared the launch pad.

Three-Stage Rocket
The *Saturn 5* rocket had three stages. Each was jettisoned (cast away) once its fuel was used up. This lightened the load to be carried upwards.

•THE LAUNCH OF APOLLO 11•

Ready for Take-Off
Dressed in bulky spacesuits, the astronauts were helped into their seats aboard *Columbia*. Then *Columbia*'s hatch was closed. Mission Control informed the astronauts: "You are go for launch."

Audience of Millions
Thousands of spectators had gathered at a safe distance to see *Apollo 11* blast off. Millions more followed the event on television or radio, as the astronauts made their final preparations for take-off.

"Three, two, one, zero… we have lift-off!" – the excited ground crew at Cape Canaveral watched as Apollo 11 rose into the air. The engines of the Saturn 5 rocket burned 15 tons of fuel per second and produced one of the loudest sounds ever heard.

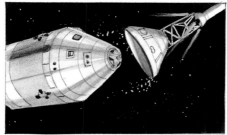

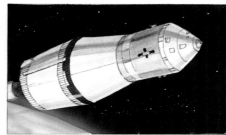

Escape Tower Jettisoned
After three minutes, the launch escape tower which had fitted over the command module was jettisoned. Now the astronauts could see out.

Third Stage Ignited
Nine minutes into the flight, the second rocket stage burnt out and was jettisoned. The third stage engines took over as the rocket roared upwards.

Into Orbit
Eleven minutes after take-off, *Apollo 11* and the third stage rocket reached Earth's orbit. Final checks were made before heading for the Moon.

•ON COURSE•

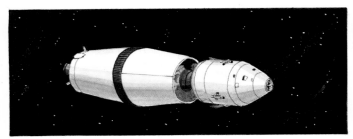

Tricky Move
Once free of Earth's orbit, command module pilot Michael Collins eased *Columbia* with the service module clear of the third stage of the *Saturn 5*. Then he turned the spacecraft around and steered back towards the rocket.

Panels Away
As *Columbia* approached, panels which had protected *Eagle* during take-off were jettisoned to reveal the flimsy craft. Not built to fly in Earth's atmosphere, the lunar module was only covered by thin layers of foil.

THREE HOURS into *Apollo 11*'s flight, Mission Control in Houston gave the astronauts permission to head for the Moon. The engines of the third stage *Saturn* rocket blasted the spacecraft free of the Earth's orbit. Then, as *Apollo* hurtled towards the Moon, Michael Collins took the center seat for a difficult maneuver. He had to disengage *Columbia* from the rocket and turn around to dock with the lunar module, which had been housed inside the third stage. Collins performed the delicate operation perfectly. Once *Eagle* had been retrieved, the third stage was left behind. The astronauts could settle down for their three-day journey to the Moon.

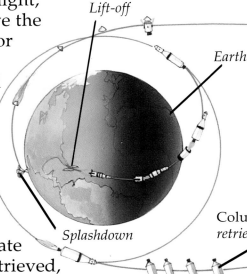

Lift-off

Earth

Splashdown

Columbia *retrieves* Eagle

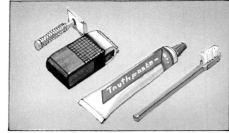

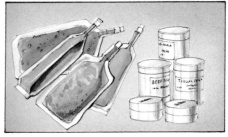

Emergency Supplies
Apollo was well stocked with supplies. Its emergency survival kit included a life raft in case the crew landed off course on Earth.

Shaving in Space
In weightless conditions, food, water, and supplies had to be well packaged or they would float away. Shaving gear was adapted for zero gravity.

Instant Food
To save on weight, food was freeze-dried and sealed in packets. A typical meal was chicken or salmon with rice, biscuit cubes, cocoa, and juice.

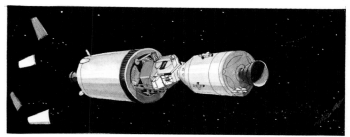

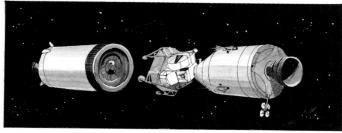

Docking

Collins maneuvered the command module of *Apollo 11* towards *Eagle* with the help of the small rocket thrusters on the sides of the service module. Then *Columbia* docked gently with the lunar module.

Leaving Earth Behind

Collins reversed *Columbia* to disengage the lunar module from the *Saturn* rocket. Then, with *Eagle* firmly attached to the nose of the command module, *Apollo 11* headed for the Moon.

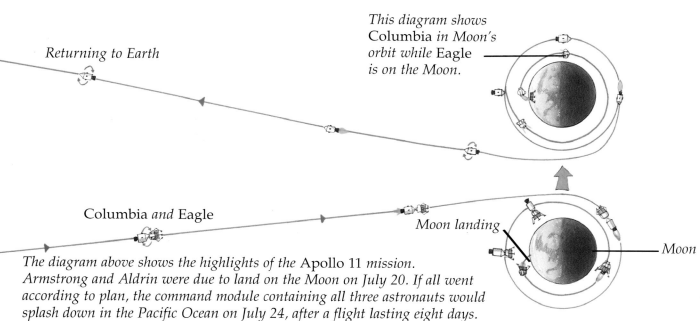

This diagram shows Columbia *in Moon's orbit while* Eagle *is on the Moon.*

Returning to Earth

Moon landing

Moon

Columbia *and* Eagle

The diagram above shows the highlights of the Apollo 11 *mission. Armstrong and Aldrin were due to land on the Moon on July 20. If all went according to plan, the command module containing all three astronauts would splash down in the Pacific Ocean on July 24, after a flight lasting eight days.*

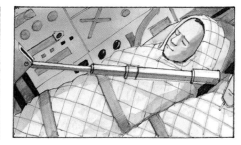

Table Manners

Hungry astronauts squirted water from a dispenser into the food packets and kneaded the bags. Then they squeezed the contents into their mouths.

Weightless Work

During the flight, a TV camera on board *Apollo 11* gave audiences on Earth a tour of the ship and showed the men working in zero gravity.

Time to Rest

During rest periods the astronauts slept in sleeping bags tied below their seats so that they would not float away across the cabin.

•TOUCHDOWN•

Into the Moon Lander
After breakfast on July 20, the astronauts, who had spent most of the trip in overalls, put on their spacesuits. Neil Armstrong and Buzz Aldrin floated through the connecting tunnel into *Eagle*, leaving Collins alone in *Columbia*.

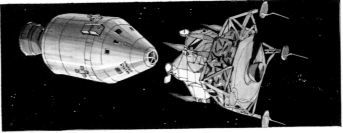

Winged Eagle
The two craft separated as they went behind the Moon again. *Columbia* continued to orbit the Moon, while *Eagle* fired its descent engine to slow down for the landing. "The *Eagle* has wings," Armstrong announced.

O N JULY 19, *Apollo 11* reached the Moon. The astronauts fired *Columbia*'s rockets to enter Moon's orbit. The next day Armstrong and Aldrin moved into the lunar module, *Eagle*, leaving Collins in charge of *Columbia*. The craft separated, and *Eagle* began its descent to the Sea of Tranquillity, the landing site. Armstrong saw that the computer was about to land the craft in a crater filled with rocks. As fuel ran low he guided *Eagle* to a more level spot, and touched down gently. The promise made by President Kennedy in 1961 had been kept. Humans had landed on the Moon.

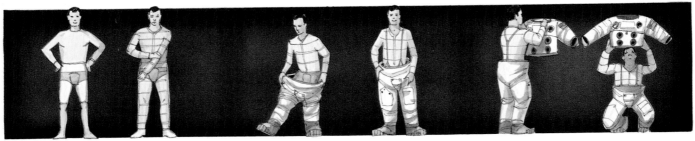

Getting Dressed
The *Apollo* astronauts wore spacesuits at critical times such as take-off and re-entry. Getting dressed was quite a lengthy process.

1. Underwear
The pressurized spacesuits were made up of several protective layers. Next to his skin each astronaut wore long underwear.

2. Extra Protection
On the Moon, Armstrong and Aldrin needed extra protection from intense heat and cold. They wore special water-cooled underwear.

• APOLLO 11 LANDS ON THE MOON •

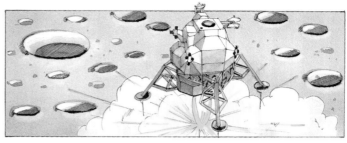

About to Land
As *Eagle* neared the surface, Armstrong spotted that they were about to land on very rough ground. If the craft tipped over, it would not be able to take off again. The two men would be stranded on the Moon.

Steered to Safety
Armstrong took over control of the landing, slowed *Eagle*'s descent and steered the craft away from the crater. But the descent engine was almost out of fuel. With seconds to spare Armstrong landed safely.

During the final moments of descent, Armstrong wrestled with the controls as Aldrin called out the craft's height and speed. Fuel ran out just as one of Eagle's *feet touched the dusty ground. There was silence, and then the ground crew heard the calm voice of Neil Armstrong: "Houston, Tranquillity Base here. The* Eagle *has landed."*

3. A Practical Suit
A large pocket on the spacesuit's leg was used for collecting rock samples. They also carried backpacks with a supply of oxygen to breathe.

4. Headgear
Each astronaut wore a soft cloth helmet with a built-in microphone and earphones so he could communicate with Mission Control.

5. Finishing Touches
A hard helmet like a goldfish bowl fitted on top. Flexible over-gloves added protection on the Moon and completed the outfit.

•ONE GIANT LEAP•

Opening the Hatch

Once on the Moon, it had been planned that the astronauts would sleep for four hours before going outside. However, they were too excited to rest. The men prepared to leave, then Armstrong opened the hatch.

D OWN AT Tranquillity Base, Armstrong and Aldrin got into their life-support units and the protective clothing they would need. Armstrong opened *Eagle*'s hatch, then stepped down onto the surface of the Moon. "That's one small step for a man, one giant leap for mankind," he said. Buzz Aldrin joined him, and the two astronauts planted the American flag. They listened to their radios as Richard Nixon, the new American president, congratulated them on the success of one of the greatest achievements of all time.

Walking on the Moon

On the Moon's surface, Armstrong and Aldrin practiced moving around in gravity one-sixth the strength of Earth's. They tried walking, bouncing, and jumping on the stony plain, but found walking worked best.

Armstrong jumped down onto the Moon.

Moonrock

The astronauts collected 48.4 pounds (22 kilograms) of rocks and soil. The rocks were found to be similar to those on Earth, but much older.

Precious Dust

When magnified, Moon dust collected from the Sea of Tranquillity was found to contain tiny pieces of glass that shine like jewels.

Left on the Moon

Footprints left on the Moon by Armstrong and Aldrin will last for thousands of years. There is no wind or rain to blow or wash them away.

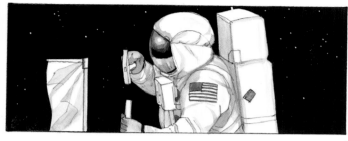

Scientific Mission
NASA scientists had given the astronauts a number of tasks to carry out on the Moon. As Armstrong filmed, Aldrin set up a metal foil strip which was used to take scientific measurements.

Taking Samples
Aldrin hammered a hollow tube into the ground to collect a sample of Moon soil which would be analyzed by scientists back on Earth. He also set up an instrument designed to measure "Moonquakes."

The astronauts spent two-and-a-half hours on the lunar surface. They set up many experiments, including a laser mirror which was used by scientists to measure the exact distance between the Earth and the Moon.

Flying the Flag
The flag planted by the astronauts was held out straight by a metal rod along the top, because there is no wind to make the flag flutter.

Medals for Space Heroes
The astronauts also left medals and badges on the Moon in memory of all those who had died during the history of space travel.

Making History
During the Moon trip Neil Armstrong uncovered a metal plaque to mark the first Moon visit. It reads "We came in peace for all mankind."

•MISSION ACCOMPLISHED•

Last to Leave
When the astronauts had completed their tasks, they returned to *Eagle*. Armstrong was the last to leave. He climbed the ladder and squeezed through the hatch. Then the hatch was closed.

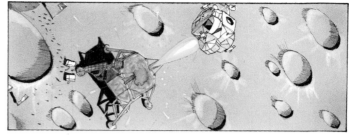

Take-Off from the Moon
Eagle's ascent rocket was the only part of the *Apollo 11* spacecraft that had no back-up system. But it fired smoothly and the little craft soared upwards towards *Columbia*, which was orbiting above to take the astronauts home.

BACK IN THE lunar module, the astronauts prepared for take-off. Aldrin fired *Eagle*'s ascent engine anxiously. If the rocket failed they would be trapped on the Moon. But all was well, and *Eagle* blasted upwards to meet *Columbia*. Reunited, the three astronauts returned to Earth in *Columbia* and splashed down safely in the Ocean. They were immediately placed in isolation, or quarantine, in case they had brought back any dangerous Moon germs. But doctors soon declared that they were all perfectly healthy.

While Armstrong and Aldrin were on the Moon, Collins orbited above in Columbia. *He was glad see his fellow astronauts when they returned.*

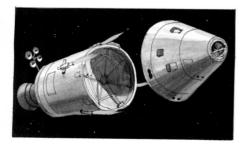

Return Trip
Apollo 11 approached the Earth at a speed of 16,200 miles (27,000 kilometers) per hour. *Columbia* then separated from the service module.

Re-Entry into the Atmosphere
Columbia was coated with a special layer to withstand the heat of re-entry. The layer burned, but inside the astronauts were safe.

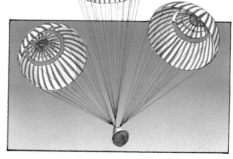

Parachutes Open
As command module *Columbia* dropped through the air, large parachutes stored in the nose cone opened to slow the spacecraft's fall.

•APOLLO 11 RETURNS TO EARTH•

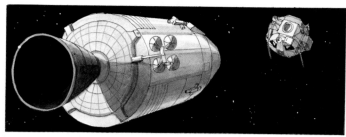

The Lonely Astronaut
Alone in *Columbia* round the far side of the Moon, Collins was out of contact with Earth and the other astronauts. A newspaper called him "the loneliest man in the universe". He watched eagerly as *Eagle* approached.

Reunited
The two craft docked successfully. Then Collins opened the connecting hatch, and Armstrong and Aldrin floated through to join him. *Eagle* was abandoned as the command module, *Columbia*, headed back to Earth.

In an isolation container on board the recovery ship, the astronauts were greeted by President Nixon. After 20 days doctors declared the astronauts fit and healthy. When their quarantine ended, they were driven through the streets of America, and cheered as heroes. They went on to tour many countries and received a heroes' welcome wherever they went.

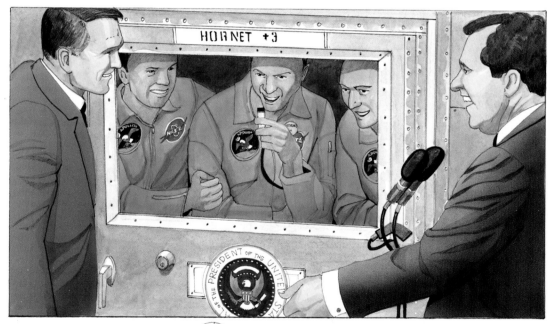

Splashdown
Columbia splashed down in the Pacific Ocean and then turned upside down. Balloons released from the nose-cone turned it the right way up.

Helicopter Rescue
As *Columbia* bobbed in the ocean, a crew from the US navy ship *Hornet* arrived in a helicopter to rescue the astronauts.

Lifted to Safety
The men were winched up into the helicopter and flown to the *Hornet*, where they entered the isolation container for their quarantine.

• THE END OF APOLLO •

Unlucky 13
Two days into the *Apollo 13* mission, an explosion badly damaged the command module's life-support system. The Moon landing was abandoned and the crew only just made it safely back to Earth.

SIX OTHER *Apollo* missions were launched after *Apollo 11*. Five were successful and landed on the moon, but *Apollo 13* was nearly a disaster. About 198,000 miles (330,000 kilometers) from Earth, an explosion on board damaged the craft. The crew had to rely on supplies of power, water, and breathable air from their lunar module as they looped around the Moon and headed back to Earth. They splashed down safely. Meanwhile the Soviet Union had concentrated on putting space stations in Earth orbit, and sending probes without cosmonauts to explore space.

The Last Apollos
In 1972, *Apollo 17* was the last mission with a crew to be sent to the Moon. Astronauts Eugene Cernan and Harrison Schmitt spent 22 hours on the Moon's surface.

In 1975 a Soviet Soyuz *craft docked with an American* Apollo *in space. The crews visited each other.*

Living in Space
Astronauts spending long periods on board space stations must exercise every day or their muscles will begin to weaken.

Taking a Bath
In zero gravity bathing is difficult, because the water tends to float away! Special showers help astronauts to keep clean in space.

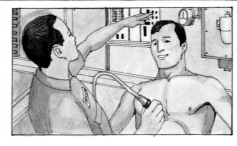

Staying Healthy
Astronauts in space for long periods can develop health problems connected with being weightless. Medical checks make sure they are fit.

•THE FINAL MOON MISSIONS•

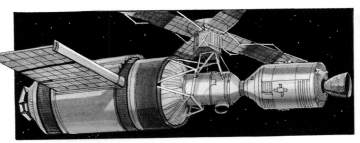

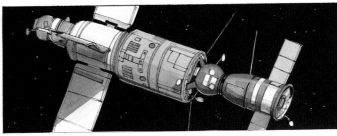

Space Stations
When the *Apollo* missions ended America concentrated on building a space station. *Skylab* was launched in 1974 but only operated for six months.

Soviet Skill
By the early 1970s the Soviet Union had gained more experience than the Americans in operating space stations. In 1974 cosmonauts spent a record 63 days in the space station *Salyut 4*.

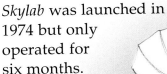

On the later Apollo *missions astronauts traveled on the Moon's surface in buggies called lunar roving vehicles. These were battery-powered and carried astronauts up to 3.6 miles (six kilometers) from the lunar module to explore and carry out experiments.*

Dangers of Space
Spacecraft orbiting high above the Earth risk being struck by showers of meteoroids. A strong double outer layer provides them with protection.

Sunscreen
Out in space it is unbearably hot in the Sun's glare, and freezing cold in the shadows. The *Skylab* crew had to rig a sunshade to protect the craft.

Space Litter
After years of space exploration, there are many dead satellites in orbit round the Earth. Spacecraft must be careful to avoid collisions!

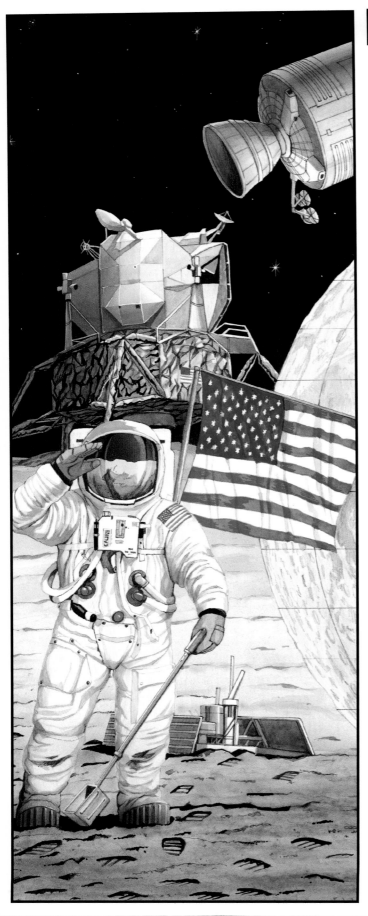

THE UNITED STATES spent enormous sums of money on the *Apollo* project. By the time the *Apollo 17* astronauts left the Moon, the project had cost a staggering $25 billion. Each expensive Apollo craft was only used once, then thrown away. In the 1980s and 1990s, both America and the Soviet Union developed reusable spacecraft, built to fly a series of missions, not just one. The Soviet Union has led in the development of space stations, and both countries have sent probes to other planets in our solar system. In recent years other countries, including China, Japan, and European nations, have also begun their own space programs.

THE SPACE SHUTTLE is America's reusable spacecraft. It was first launched in 1981. It launches like a rocket, with the aid of strap-on booster rockets and a large main fuel tank, which is jettisoned soon after take-off.

The shuttle carries new satellites into orbit. It may also carry up to seven astronauts on board. They may leave the craft in spacesuits to repair satellites and other space equipment. Outside the craft, astronauts move around using a Manned Maneuvering Unit (MMU), a pack containing a life-support system and gas jets for moving around.

In 1992 American astronauts spent eight hours in space repairing the communications satellite *Intelsat 6*. When the shuttle's tasks are done, it returns to Earth and lands on a runway, like an aeroplane. Within two weeks it may be ready for another mission. The shuttle project has been mostly successful, although it had a major setback in 1986. Just after lift-off, the shuttle *Challenger* caught fire and exploded, killing all seven crew members. After this disaster, the project was re-examined carefully to find out what had gone wrong and to make sure it never happened again.

AFTER SUCCESS with early prototype space stations, the Soviet Union launched space station *Mir* in 1986. Since then *Mir* has been occupied continuously by different crews who spend months in space doing research. Soviet cosmonauts have set the records for the longest periods spent in space. Yuri Romanenko spent over a year in space, on three separate missions.

SINCE THE 1970s, probes without crews have revealed many of the secrets of our solar system. The American probe *Mariner 2* was first to visit another planet, Venus, in 1962. *Mariner 9* orbited Mars. *Voyagers 1* and 2 were launched in 1977. They visited Jupiter, Saturn, and Uranus and then left the solar system. They are still sending back signals. The Hubble space telescope was launched in 1990 and repaired by astronauts in 1993. Orbiting high above the Earth, this powerful, giant telescope sends back the clearest pictures yet of distant stars out in deep space.

•GLOSSARY•

Altitude
Height, usually above sea level.

Atmosphere
A layer of gases, including oxygen, surrounding the Earth.

Booster
A rocket engine strapped to a spacecraft which gives a short burst of extra power, particularly during take-off.

Cosmonaut
The Russian word for astronaut.

Docking
The linking of two craft in space.

G force
A measure of the force of gravity.

Jettison
To release or throw away.

Liquid fuel
A fuel normally in gas form, but which has been made into liquid through extreme cooling.

Lunar
Relating to the Moon.

Maneuver
A planned movement, or to move.

Module
A section of a spacecraft.

Orbit
The curved path of one object circling another.

Probe
A small craft not built to carry human passengers.

Prototype
An original model.

Quarantine
A period passed in isolation, for health reasons.

Re-entry
The return of a spacecraft to Earth's atmosphere.

Satellite
An object circling a larger body in space, such as a planet. The Moon is a satellite of the Earth.

Simulator
A machine built to imitate the conditions of another environment.

Splashdown
A sea-landing after a space flight.

Stage
A section of a rocket.

Thrust
The pushing power produced by a rocket's engine.

Thruster
A small rocket motor used by a spacecraft to maneuver.

Zero gravity
The condition of weightlessness that exists beyond the pull of gravity.

INDEX